TRAIN LIKE YOU FIGHT

Today's Preparation for Tomorrow's Mission

By

Terry "Ranger" Johnson

ChampionsWithin Kingdom Builders

ISBN-13:978-0692111260

Published By:
ChampionsWithin Kingdom Builders
Publishing Company
Website: www.rangerjohnson.com

"Train while they sleep.
Learn while they lounge.
Invest while they bury.
Live like they dream."

-Terry "Ranger" Johnson

"Your gift will make room for you..."
Proverbs 18:16

Prepared for the Mission..

ENDORSEMENTS

Terry Johnson is a phenomenal speaker. He has motivated many people to pursue their purpose including myself. His programs have helped me to unlock the hidden gifts within myself. Keep doing what you do because "YOU WERE BORN TO WIN- STEP UP".

Jordan Hirsch, CEO
JHSpeaks Enterprise,LLC

Ranger is an absolutely amazing writer, speaker, and facilitator! More remarkable is Ranger's passion and person!! His ability to promote a spirit of excellence without excuse is contagious! We were blessed to have Ranger as a guest speaker!!!

Sidney K. Mitchell, Ph.D.

-Ranger Johnson is a very powerful, passionate speaker.
-Ranger Johnson's ability to connect with each student during each session was very impressive.
-Ranger Johnson's energy level and enthusiasm kept our attention the entire time.

IMAGE PROGRAM- Students
University of Mississippi

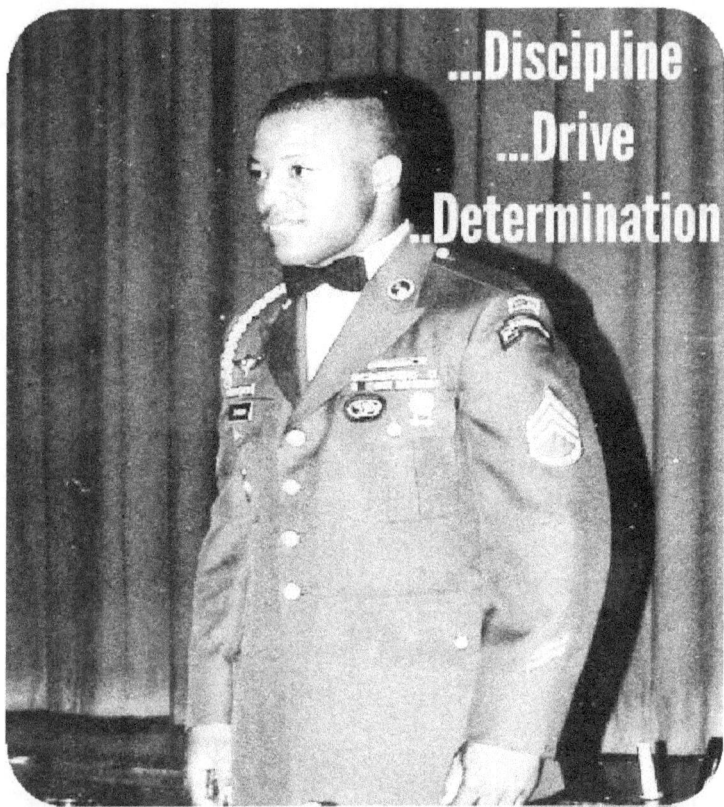

...Discipline
...Drive
..Determination

CONTENTS

DEDICATION

This book is dedicated to the ones who have played a significant part in every scene of my journey and lit a fire under me to pursue greatness. My Mentor: The Late **CSM Mike Jefferson,** My Grandparents: The Late **Ralph and Winnie Lockett**, My In-Laws: The Late **Rev. Willie and Orleana Minor**, My Parents: **Eymitine Whitmore and Terry G. Johnson;** and last but not least, my wife and Proverbs 31 Queen-**Renee Minor Johnson.** My amazing bride has been with me through thick and thin and continues to believe in me beyond what my eyes can see. I am more than grateful to God for all of the seeds that have been planted and watered in my life.

...one who waters will himself be watered.
Proverbs 11:25

FOREWORD

Terry Johnson, or (Coach) as I like to refer to him, is a positive force. I can recall the first time I met him in 2011 at an outdoor concert on the campus of the University of Mississippi. I actually heard him coming before I saw him. Just from hearing his voice I could tell I was about to meet someone special. He introduced himself, and so did I. We have been friends and professional colleagues since.

I was thrilled to learn that Coach was becoming a member of our church. From that point on we collaborated on several projects. It was mostly I assisting him with his "Champions Within" programs either as a recording engineer or performing on my steel drum for his events. He invited me to assist with programs for organizations like Leflore County H.S., Caterpillar, Inc., and the University of Mississippi to name a few. We even joined forces in presenting a Black History Month concert at our church.

9

Terry is a well-rounded individual and an experienced teacher/motivator. He is hard working, diligent, and strives for excellence. I have observed him to be well organized, knowledgeable and current in topics dealing with motivation, empowerment and finding your calling. He has extensive experience in team building and is living proof of a country boy who has highly achieved. He is passionate about his work and is committed to helping people succeed in life.

Ricky Burkhead
Professor of Music and Director of Percussion
University of Mississippi
Roster Artist for Mississippi Arts Commission
rickyburkhead.com
www.facebook.com/ricky.burkhead

INTRODUCTION

Everybody wants to eat, but few people are willing to hunt. Many people have a desire to be great, but not many are willing to put in the work. We all have the capacity to dream, but doing the work to bring it to life requires fight. Steve Harvey said, **"The dream is free, but the hustle is sold separately."** Desire and hunger... connected with preparation and fight, equals **success**. Train like you fight today for victory tomorrow.

In the title of this book, "Train Like You Fight," the word fight is only used as a modifier. You see, in this game of life, you will face some tough situations... situations that you may not believe you can overcome; however, if you **prepare** for the game with the same tenacity as **playing** the game... you will win. You've been equipped with everything you need to succeed. You, and I can do all things through Christ. Yes,

He is the one who strengthens us. The training manual of God's Word is filled with strategies to help us prepare for life's battles.

He calls us VICTORIOUS!!

When we train like we fight, we are merely preparing today for tomorrow's assignment. The concepts, precepts, and ideas shared in this book are not based on humanism, psychology, or philosophy. This insight has been downloaded from God for preparing us for the journey ahead. It is written in Ephesians 2:10 that we are created for good works which God **prepared for us** beforehand. In other words, the foundation was laid inclusive of our assignments. God had and still has a plan for every gift planted within us. He has clearly laid out everything in His Word for us as training material to prepare us for the upcoming missions. This is the strategy of a soldier!!

"Preparation precedes success on every level.."

Benjamin Franklin once said, "By failing to prepare, you are preparing to fail." I hope you will feel renewed, empowered, and catch a fresh wind beneath your wings, enabling you to soar higher and achieve great things. Moreover, I pray that you will place your trust in God and allow the Holy Spirit to impart wisdom and revelation to prepare you for significant tasks.

Every morning presents a new opportunity for us to strive for excellence, reach for greater heights, and dream bigger. Let's not squander this chance; let's go for it. It's a tremendous privilege for me to share these thoughts with you. The goal of writing this book is not to overwhelm you with new knowledge, but to reaffirm what you already know about yourself. You were born to succeed, but life's challenges can sometimes hinder that. In those moments, we can choose to fight back or give up. Many people have sacrificed their lives for the privileges we enjoy today. So, let's make the most of every moment while we still have breath in our bodies. Time is still ticking and it is precious.

My purpose is and must always be pointed toward fulfilling God's Mission. Completing this book was one of my many assignments. It has been said that today's excuses lead to tomorrow's regrets. Upon completing this book, I pray that your hunger to win will push you to bury the excuses and to train like you fight by preparing today for tomorrow's mission. Let's finish our race with **fervency...**

"NO REGRETS"

**If discipline,
drive, and determination
Is your mantra,
Victory will be your outcome!!
-Terry "Ranger" Johnson**

CHAPTER 1

TRAIN FOR THE MISSION

Throughout my 55-plus years of living, one key lesson stands out: training like you fight can change the trajectory of your life. In February 1987, I reported to one of the toughest and most elite units in the U.S. Army, the 1/75th Ranger Battalion at Hunter Army Airfield in Savannah, Georgia. Upon arriving at my assigned unit, I immediately felt out of place. As a young black soldier in one of the military's most challenging units, I was one of the few soldiers who looked like me. Despite entering the unit with medals, stripes, and honors, my comfort zone was profoundly challenged.

As I stood across from my First Sergeant, I noticed a look of concern in his eyes. This look of concern was followed by his statement, "Well, Sgt. Johnson, you're here now. Let me see where we are going to put you." For the first time in my life, I truly felt like an outsider—an alien in my own country. To be prepared for tomorrow's mission, I had to move past this place of discomfort. It was a significant hurdle I had to overcome. I also had to ask myself an important question: "Was it about my First Sergeant, or was it about me?"

After being in the Ranger Battalion a few months, one of the platoon sergeants told me a warrior's story that I will never forget. He said "Terry, man I know how you feel coming to this unit and being one of the few black men here.

I was a golden gloves boxer, but every time I stepped in the gym, I felt the same type of stares that you get. It seemed as though brothers were saying…"Here comes some easy meat; let me knock this white boy out. In my mind, the only way I could earn their respect was to knock some guys out, and that's what I did." He proceeded to say "Terry, **just soldier** and **perform**. You will find that your standout performance cannot be denied." I am so very thankful to that fellow soldier who passionately encouraged me to **JUST SOLDIER**. Wouldn't it be great if we made it a mandate to encourage someone to go beyond their thoughts and ideas in pursuit of their dreams and visions?

I once read a powerful quote by author Larry Crabb, who said, "A vision we give to others of who and what they could become has power when it echoes what the Spirit has already spoken into their souls." An encouraging word and a renewed mind have the potential to transform our lives.

Being part of the 1/75th Ranger Battalion was one of the most exciting experiences in my life. It was truly a dream come true. Although it was not without challenges, I grasped the power of mental and physical preparation. I have served alongside many great warriors, leaders, and mentors; I will always have an enormous amount of honor and respect for them.

The Enemy of Comfort

As human beings, we prefer not to be uncomfortable or pushed past our limits. Unfortunately, continuous comfort can lull us to sleep, causing us to miss out on open doors of opportunities. Allow me to paint a picture...

Have you ever eaten dinner on a Sunday afternoon and decided to sit in the recliner to watch a football game? Then, you fell asleep... only to be awakened by the 6"o clock news and the **game was over** the comfort of a full stomach and a soft recliner lulled you to sleep. That is a good example of the enemy of comfort. When we are not willing to push beyond our comforts and limitations, we will wake up and this game called life will be over. My message to you is this, "Pursue your dreams and don't allow opportunities to pass you by because of the "enemy of comfort."

The purpose of training is to form a habit that comes naturally when it's game time. I call it "unconscious competence". Now, let's talk habits. Some say one can create a habit in 21 days; whether true or false, I do know that it is easier to start a new habit than it is to break an old one. More than 40 years ago, I formed a habit of working out 3 to 5 times a week. Due to service injuries, my workouts have been slightly modified. My military background can be attributed to my workout **habits**.

Our success or failure in life is linked to our habits. The actions we consistently take will become either good or bad habits. This may sound like a simple comparison, but many people overlook its significance. Our habits may be so integrated into our daily routine that we fail to notice them. I perceive habits as a clandestine Special Forces assault team, you never know they are there until it's too late. The right training produces the right habit for the mission ahead. You were created to solve a problem so push past your discomfort and make the decision to train for the mission. **The world is waiting on you!!**

"Comfort is the assassin of greatness"...

Have you ever been at your "assigned place" but felt out of place? Explain:

_____

_____

_____

_____

_____

_____

_____

How did you handle it?

_____

_____

_____

_____

_____

_____

_____

Fast forward... How would you handle it if you faced the same situation today?

_____

_____

_____

_____

_____

_____

CHAPTER 2

THE POWER OF A DREAM

I believe that our dreams and visions are somehow connected to the gifts and talents that have been planted within us. I hope and pray that during this passage every dormant gift inside of you will be quickened. The importance of working in your God-given gift should never be underestimated. There are so many life situations that have the potential to throw you off track as you drive closer to your dreams; however, your passion and your hunger to succeed has the magnetic ability to pull you into your destiny. My desire is to push, motivate, and simply move you toward chasing your dreams as if they were a lost treasure.

Everyone should have a dream box and every dream box requires fuel to keep dreams alive. The power inside your dream box will move you to incredible heights of victory and success. The inner fire that is tied to your destiny will get you as excited as a 5 year- old on Christmas morning. So, if you find that you are lacking that fire, and wondering why you are not excited about your life, the answer could be that you probably have not looked inside your dream box lately. You may need to have your fire stoked. Let's talk more about the dream box.

A dream box is not something that would be nice have. A dream box is a necessity. A dream box and faith walk should go hand-in-hand. It's our **contribution to the world**. What will you contribute to this world? My father- in-law would ask this question, "Are you a contributor or a consumer?" Will this world be better because you came? Let me go deeper.

I don't believe material possessions will ever be enough to keep us going when things get tough. What keeps me going during the tough times is understanding this..."God created me with and for a purpose." I was created to solve a problem on this earth and so were you. We all have a God imparted uniqueness. By God's design you are one of a kind. Looking deeper into our dreambox we will find that the passion to stay in the fight is deeply connected to us being... **"the answer to a problem"**. Passion and purpose breathe life into our dream box, so take inventory of your gift/s and start

cultivating your strongest gift to not only

achieve your goals but to also help others

achieve theirs. So, now I ask..."what are you

doing with the dreams in your dream box?" The

clock is ticking, and time is valuable.

What Are You Doing Now?

It matters not if you lost the fight and were badly beaten too.
It matters not if you failed outright in the things you tried to do.

It matters not if you toppled down from the azure heights of blue,
But what are you doing now???

It matters not if your plans were foiled and your hopes have fallen through.
It matters not if your chance was spoiled for the gain almost in view.

It matters not if you missed the goal though you struggled brave and true... But what are you doing now???

It matters not if your fortune's gone and your fame has vanished too.

It matters not if a cruel world's score be directed straight at you.
It matters not if the worst has come and your dreams have not come true...But what are you doing now????
-R. Rhodes Stabley

Are you pursuing the dreams in your dream box?

_____

Why? What are you doing now?

_____

_____

_____

_____

"Change Hurts, but staying the same hurts even worst" ...
-Dave Ramsey

TODAY'S PREPARATION

_____

_____

_____

_____

_____

_____

_____

_____

_____

_____

_____

CHAPTER 3

TIME IS VALUABLE

Time is valuable and as fleeting as our thoughts. We are only here on this earth, for a brief moment so what we do while we are here matters. With that being said, let me pose these questions? "How will you spend the rest of your time on this side of eternity?" "What will be your legacy?" Being a boy from the south (**East Texas**) I grew up listening to many people say that they were "fixin' to do something". **Fixin' to,** is an old southern term meaning, "about to do, or going to do, something". What I have so often observed is this..."**fixin' to**" never gets done. So, how do we go from **"fixin' to"** to doing???

I don't believe this book has all the answers; however, I do believe that as you read it and allow your mind to be renewed during the process, the eyes of your understanding will be enlightened. James 1:22(TPT) says it best... "Don't just listen to the Word of Truth and not respond to it, for that is the essence of self-deception. Therefore, let His Word become like poetry written and fulfilled by your life! In other words, we should be more than hearers, we should be doers!!!

What Is Your Gift?

Proverbs 18:16 says, "A man's gift makes room for him, and brings him before great men. This one bible verse gave me so much power and encouragement. Reading this verse was like throwing wood on a smoldering fire...

it set me ablaze. I knew there was more for me to do on my earth journey and I always felt I would do something great... however, I didn't know how to get the ball rolling. I didn't realize that my military career was preparing me for assignments down the road. I want you to understand that right where you are is preparation ground as you move toward your destiny. Know this, time is our most valuable asset. Begin to get excited about the life God has given you and the possibilities ahead. Take inventory of your gifts and abilities and infuse those talents with positive energy to be a game changer. Time is valuable and positive energy is contagious. Either we affect people or infect people... **Let's affect the KINGDOM!!!!**

"Time is our most valuable asset" ...

Prepare with Passion

I believe your destiny path will come through your gift and your gift will determine your legacy. A major key in this factor is to work it with passion. You must be determined to win no matter what if you want to leave a legacy...I have yet to find a successful person, in any field, that has not worked hard to build a strong organization, ministry, marriage... etc. Winning or succeeding at any level requires preparation... Success doesn't respond to lukewarm passion. Lukewarm passion and lukewarm preparation will never be enough to complete the mission.

...It's Inside of You

Everything that you need to succeed is already inside of you. For many years I searched for the right job, or the right situation to come my way in pursuit of success. Although I see myself as a certified dreamer, I quickly found out that if I wasn't persistent and constant, in feeding my dreams, I would easily fall into a state of hopelessness. One day as I was reading my Bible the Holy Spirit revealed to me that He had given me everything that I needed to become successful. 2 Peter 1:3 came alive... it read, "the Lord has given us everything that is necessary for living the truly good life, in allowing us to know the one who has called us to Him, through His own glorious goodness." At that point, I had no more excuses; this became my mantra..."**Stay in the fight**". With a renewed mind, I assessed my situation and stopped looking around me and began looking within me..."**The Champion Within**"..

So often we are looking all around us for something that we already possess. This reminds me of an interesting story titled...

"Acres of Diamonds" by Russell Conwell. Acers of Diamonds is the story of a wayward farmer who sold his farm and went out in search of his dreams to find diamonds in South Africa during the diamond rush. The farmer searched and searched but couldn't find the type of diamonds that he felt would give him wealth, and riches... In a fit of despondency, the farmer threw himself into a river and drowned. Sometime later, a new farmer was walking across a creek on the property of the wayward farmer and he noticed a shiny large rock in the bottom of a creek bed. The farmer picked up the shiny rock to observe its beauty and became captivated by its glow. He quickly rushed the shiny rock back to his house and made a special place for it on the mantle, above the fireplace. One day an old friend stopped by to visit the farmer and noticed the shiny rock on the mantle. He asked him where he found it. The farmer replied, "I found that rock in my creek bed, and there are many more where that one came from... maybe not as big, but they are plentiful." That **"rock"** turned out to be one of the largest diamonds in the world and the wayward farmer had owned it free and clear. The wayward farmer gave up on his dream and lost it all in a moment of despair... He failed to realize that his dreams were within his reach all along. Needless to say, the new farmer became, wealthy (rich and famous). Please don't rushto be overly critical of the wayward farmer. If you were totally honest with yourself, at one time you probably felt or thought like the wayward farmer. Sometimes we have a tendency to think someone else has been given a better road map to success or others have beendealt a better hand than us. Well, I came to tell you that we possess diamonds within us... we have everything we need to win. So, to retreat or to surrender, is not an option. Don't allow fear of failure to stand between you and your dreams. Remember, every obstacle brings forth opportunity... so, take advantage of your opportunities and start today rebuilding your dreams. "The fear of failure, coupled with procrastination, are silent dream killers."

The longer you put off pursuing your dreams,

THE HARDER IT IS TO MOVE FORWARD.

Remove the fear of failure and LET'S

ATTACK!!!!

"Failure is another stepping-stone to greatness" ... Oprah Winfrey

"Procrastination is the thief of success" -Unknown

What is your gift?

_____

_____

_____

_____

_____

Are you afraid of using your gift?

_____

_____

_____

What are you passionate about?

_____

_____

_____

_____

How can using your gift/talent help others?

_____

_____

_____

_____

"No one will believe in you until you believe in you" ...

TODAY'S PREPARATION

_____

_____

_____

_____

_____

_____

_____

_____

_____

_____

_____

Think you can...Dream you can...Believe you

will...**Make it happen!!**

THINK

DREAM

BELIEVE

CHAPTER 4

REBUILD YOUR DREAM

It is never too late to rebuild your dreams. So often we are lulled to sleep by comfort and we sleep longer than planned. The calmness of sleep and the inactivity has now awakened to a living nightmare leading you to believe it is too late to begin again or to dream again. Well, let me encourage you, it is never too late todream again... Let me give you a few ideas on how to move forward in rebuilding your dreams.

Please understand that success is more than money. Earl Nightingale gave one of the best definitions for the word success. He said "success is the pursuit of a worthy goal". I love this definition because it cuts to the chase and makes success obtainable for anyone who is willing to go for it. But please understand, in order for us to get to the place we call success we must be willing to jump in beyond the low, shallow waters. In other words, you have to be committed to swim through shark infested waters to rescue your dreams. Becoming a part of an elite (Rangers) unit in the Army was that committed place for me. What are you willing to swim through to rescue your biggest dreams? I made up my mind to complete my mission as a soldier; I retired after 20 years. Everything that I gained from my military career has helped me to become a better father, a better husband, and a better leader. I was preparing then, for my mission's today. It is not too late for you to begin preparation for tomorrow. Don't become paralyzed by comfort. New life begins at the end of comfort.

During speaking events, I often tell this crazy story of how easy it is to become paralyzed by comfort. Let me explain... I start by asking the question..."Does anyone know how to cook a bullfrog?" At that point, I proceed to explain...If you were to take that bullfrog and drop him in a pot of boiling water he would jump out. Why? The water would be too hot, but, if you take that old bull frog and put him In a pot of lukewarm water, he would become very comfortable and begin to lay back and relax. You see, the bullfrog is pretty much like us. When we finished high school, we had amazing dreams and goals that we desired to accomplish. As time passed, the lukewarm comfort/compromise set in. Yep, bit by bit, we can easily fall into the old bull frog mentality and settle for less than desired. In the midst of the beauty of marriage, children, mortgage, and car notes, we lose our focus, our dreams, and our vision. We get very comfortable... and just like the bullfrog, <u>we</u> <u>get cooked!!!</u> Comfort can rob you of your dreams like a thief in the night. Les Brown is one of my favorite speakers and he has a phrase, "You got to be hungry"!! He believes that hunger for greatness keeps us out of our comfort zone and I agree. I have found that the best way to maintain hunger is to have my goals written down; I make it a point to look at them daily... EVERY DAY!!

Habakkuk 2:2(MSG) says,

"Write this. Write what you see. Write it out in big block letters so that it can be read on the run. This vision-message is a witness pointing to what's coming. It aches for the coming—it can hardly wait! And it doesn't lie. If it seems slow in coming, wait. It's on its way. It will come right on time"...

The book of Genesis chapters 37-50 talk about Joseph's dreams. Though a lot of adversity transpired between the dream and its fruition, his dreams came forth. So, don't give up!!

NOW, let's get started on rebuilding your dreams. Get a sheet of paper and do what is called brainstorming. **Henry O. Dormann said, "A minute of thought is worth more than an hour of talk"**. Now, write down every dream that comes to mind as fast as you can. Don't worry about spelling just let your mind, body, and soul, get into the dream-scape process. After you have your dreams written down get a mental picture of how they look, taste, feel, and smell. You may also want to go get a few pictures of your biggest dreams and place them on your refrigerator door or vanity mirror. Figure out what you will have to produce in your life to make this happen. Don't get tricked and start focusing on the money. Focus on the service or job that you will do for society and society will pay you back. People don't plan to fail they fail to plan. Only 3 out of 100 people plan their day. This is why the same 3% are more success- ful than the 97% combined. Get passionate about your dreams, no one will believe in you until you believe in you.

The greatest thing about dreams is that they cost us nothing... "Dreams are free", and you can dream as big as you want. I encourage, challenge, and implore you to stop, and write down your dreams, and feed them daily. Get to work...DO IT NOW!!!

**"If you feed your dreams
your dreams will feed you back"..**

DREAM BOARD

_____

_____

_____

_____

_____

A dream doesn't become reality through magic: it takes sweat, determination, and hard work.
-Colin Powell

TODAY'S PREPARATION

_____

_____

_____

_____

_____

_____

_____

_____

_____

_____

_____

CHAPTER 5

WORK YOUR DREAM

In one of my wife's books, she has a poem titled "Feed Your Dreams." One of the quotes in the poem says, "A dream without a plan is a hallucination and all talk with no plans is just a conversation." Wow...I couldn't have said it better myself. We must become more than talkers; we have to become doers. Becoming a doer is paramount. The "doing" happens in the training process. You can't wait until you get on the battlefield to become a doer.

I love what the great motivator Les Brown says in his book Live Your Dreams, "dare to break through barriers, to find your own path." That is an awesome statement. I believe Mr.

Brown knows what he is talking about because you must be mentally tough to climb the mountains of life. You must become totally unstoppable. In my psyche, being unstoppable means training everyday as though you are already there!!! Make up your mind right now that you will get it done no matter how long it takes.

I am always amazed when someone tells me that they are too old or too young to do something. My normal response to this statement is to ask them this... "do you plan on living for the next 5 to 10 years"? ... Most of them will say yes. "Well, if you are going to live the next 5 to 10 years, would you rather have the lifestyle connected to the dreams in your dream box or the lifestyle that you have now"? So, why not

work your dream? Please, remember this,

"dreaming without doing is hallucinating... "

There is a price to be paid for greatness.

Greatness lives in the zone of the unknown. A

few years ago, NIKE had a commercial with

people saying, "I WANT TO BE LIKE MIKE".

Michael Jordan is the greatest NBA player (in

my mind) to ever play the game. As I watched

the commercial I wondered, "do they really

want to be like Mike or do they want Mikes

money and fame. Would they be willing to put

in the countless hours of work(training,practice,

watching film...etc.) to get Jordan's results?

I don't believe that many people are truly

willing to "work like Mike" to "be like Mike", in

any field (not just professional basketball). I use the word **"<u>willing</u>"** because it carries a lot of weight. The Word says that if we are willing and obedient we will eat the good of the land. That is all I need to understand the power of being "willing" to put in the work. The blessing of the benefits proceeds the willingness. Many say, "I can", but only a few will commit to "I will". Let me go a little further.

I am a sports fan, and when watching a basketball or football game, it frustrates me to see players wait until the 4th quarter to perform at their maximum level. Why save your potential? Why not decide to give your all from the start? Og Mandino said, **"I will strain my potential until it cries for mercy."** Wow...

I'm getting stirred up just thinking about this statement. So now, I ask you, "are you **ready to give it your all today? What are you waiting on? When will you decide to go for it?**" As for me..."**I would rather burn out than rust out**" ...!!!

Most people are rusting out and dying, full of potential, but not willing to use it. I don't want to take one dream to the grave with me. Wow, what an awesome thought, to complete all of your dreams and die on empty, with a smile of gratitude on your face. Don't let defeat overtake you. Stay in the fight!!!!

**When defeat overtakes a man,
the easiest and most logical thing
to do is to quit.**

-NAPOLEON HILL

THINK & GROW RICH

Failure is never final as long as you have air in your lungs and a dream in your heart. I once heard a minister say, "the enemy is the inner me". This means that we can be our own worst enemy. This statement is true when it comes to motivating yourself to take a chance on learning a new skill or getting out of your comfort zone. Sometimes life will put us in some tough situations, but we will win if we don't quit.

Galatians 6:9-10 (MSG) says, "So let's not allow ourselves to get fatigued doing good. At the right time we will harvest a good crop if we don't give up or quit. Right now, therefore every time we get the chance, let us work for the benefit of all, starting with the people closest to us in the community of faith.

How many farmers can harvest a crop that has not been planted? In this world there is no such thing as a free ride. **Greatness** has a price tag attached to it in the form of hard work and

dedication. Make up your mind today! Decide

right now that you are going to consistently pay

the price. I've learned that success won't come

from what we do occasionally... success only

comes from what we do consistently....C.O.T.

-CONSISTENCY

- OVER

-TIME.......

Am I willing to plan my work and work my plan hourly, daily, weekly or whenever is necessary? Yes / No / Why?

_____

_____

_____

_____

_____

_____

What adjustments are you willing to make in order to stay on course?

_____

_____

_____

Our forefathers paid a tremendous price for us to have the opportunity to create something great in our lives. They set the example of preparing today for tomorrow's mission. We are the benefactors of what they did hundreds of years ago. The way has been made. It is time to go to work—work your dream! No one stands in front of a fireplace and says, "Fire, give me warmth and I'll give you wood." NO—NO—NO, you have to put the wood in first before you can get the fire.

<u>REPEAT AFTER ME:</u>

I WILL PAY THE PRICE NOW,
I WILL ENDURE..

I WILL PAY THE PRICE UP FRONT...
I WILL ENDURE THE PROCESS,

AND POSSESS THE PROMISE!!!

TODAY'S PREPARATION

_____

_____

_____

_____

_____

_____

_____

_____

CHAPTER 6

SEE IT BEFORE YOU SEE IT

Many years ago, my family and I were driving back from church when we noticed a few bricks going up on the side of the road. Every Sunday afternoon, as we passed by this spot, we saw a few more bricks added to this "THING" that appeared to have no purpose. As we continued to pass this spot Sunday after Sunday, my children and I started making jokes about how strange it was to put these nice bricks up in a field, in front of an old fish pond. Now, please understand that this was over about a two-year period. For two years, the only thing we saw were two columns of bricks...

bricks. The family joke was "what a smart person to put these bricks in this old field by this old fish pond." Well, about the third year we noticed something... they started to pour a foundation for a house... a really "BIG HOUSE". By that time my curiosity had gotten the best of me and I had to ask a local business man if they knew what was happening on that piece of land. To our surprise, he said "Yes one of the biggest restaurant owners in town is building a "2 Million Dollar" home out there." Yes, we were laughing at the bricks, but we couldn't see their dream. How many people are laughing at your dreams right now? That restaurant owner saw his dream before we saw it... What an eye-opening revelation!!!

I remember my Army career coming to an end and I understood that I needed to prepare for life after camouflage and dress greens. I began my journey of becoming a businessman. One day I came into my unit wearing my suit and tie and one of my army buddies just stood there and laughed at me, he said... "Terry, how long have you been in that business?" "How much money have you made"? Yes, that's right, "my army buddy" couldn't see my dream just like we couldn't see the restaurant owners dream. There will always be dream killers and naysayers around to throw water on your fire. Some will be friends or family members, and some will be total strangers passing by. No matter the case... let neither steal your dream... They can't see it. When you know, in your knower, that you have what it takes to win, your fire can never be put out. That's the point of no return. Please repeat after me...

... **"YOU CAN'T SEE MY DREAM!!!!**

Point Of No Return

When I was going through the Special Forces Qualification Course (SFQC) at Fort Bragg, NC the instructors taught us that once you get to a certain point on a mission there is no way you can return to your base camp without completing it. This type of thinking creates a "must win" mindset that separates you from those people that choose to just float through life undirected and misguided. I truly believe we all should have a "Point of No Return" mentality. This is the point where you refuse to be denied of your God-given right to be great, to succeed, and to live the abundant life God has given us. Wow, I'm being stirred up even as I write because words have power.

In 1980 I joined the Army because I wanted to see the world and learn from the Master of Leadership. I can remember sitting on the airplane in Shreveport, LA thinking to myself that my life was about to change for the better. I have yet to look back or regret my decision to join the military because the experience helped create the dreamer in me. I am grateful for the many opportunities that have been bestowed upon me during and after my military career. I have traveled to 14 different countries, learned a foreign language, and developed into a leader who develops other leaders. I smile when I tell people that I retired with 20 years in the Army. They usually reply... "Thank you for your service. And I think to myself, "No, I'm the one that is thankful". The military and the heroic leaders that went before me gave me this opportunity. If you give me credit for anything, just say that I didn't quit!! I refused to get distracted, look back or turn around. My desire for great-ness placed a demand on my priorities so I stayed the course. **I made it past the point of... "No Return" !!**

"Distraction is the destruction of your dream in slow motion" ...
-Bishop Dale Bronner

Desire

The story is told of Roman general Julius Caesar who was about to send his reluctant soldiers into a battle with the opposition, whose men outnumbered his own. The general knew that in order to ensure the success of his army he had to develop within his men an imperative desire to win. He loaded his soldiers into boats and sailed to the enemy's land. After his troops disembarked on the enemy's shore with their equipment and artillery, the general then gave the order to burn the ships that had carried them. There on the hostile shore the soldiers watched as the red tongues of fire consumed every ship in which they had crossed. Turning to his men the general said, "You see our ships going up in smoke. With the last means of retreating burned, there is but one thing left for us to do. We cannot leave these shores alive unless we win!"
That's exactly what they did.

Alexander Lockhart
The Portable Pep Talk

Are you easily distracted?

_____

_____

_____

Have you reached your "Point of No Return?"

_____

_____

_____

_____

What happened to get you to that point?

_____

_____

_____

_____

_____

_____

Are you a dreamer?

_____

_____

_____

_____

Do you believe you have what it takes to win?

_____

_____

_____

_____

_____

_____

Always remember, you have within you
the strength, the patience, and the
passion to reach for the stars
to change the world...
-Harriet Tubman

TODAY'S PREPARATION

_____

_____

_____

_____

_____

_____

_____

_____

_____

_____

_____

_____

_____

CHAPTER 7

GIANT KILLERS

As a soldier, one of my favorite Bible stories is David and Goliath. I love this story because it brings to light this statement: "It doesn't matter the size of the dog in the fight... what matters is the size of the fight in the dog." David was the smaller dog in the fight, but his tenacity, faith, and preparation made him victorious. He was a giant killer. Although Goliath was a visible giant, some of our invisible giants are just as large. David had a plan. He relied on his faith in God, his past experiences as a shepherd defending his flock, and his skills with a sling. This story reminds us that with faith, preparation, and determination, we can overcome the giants in our lives, no matter how insurmountable they may seem.

So, what are some **invisible giants**? Fears, procrastination, adopting limitations of others as our own, low self-esteem, are a few invisible giants. Before I go further, take a minute and ponder some of the invisible giants in your life.

Early in my military career, I faced a couple of Giants. Fear and adopting my mom's limitations as my own almost stopped my pursuit of one of my biggest dreams... "**Becoming a U.S. Army Ranger**" ... and the fear of water was the giant that started it all. Let me tell you the story that helped turn my life around. Learning to swim was the toughest things I've ever done, but it gave me courage to step outside of my mental boundaries and achieve something great.

I grew up in a small Northeast Texas town called Marietta. At that time, the population of my hometown was under 115 people—yes, you got it, less than 115. My mother was so afraid of the water that she would freak out even about bath water (smile). Every time my family went to the lake, I could hear her saying, "Wendell (my middle name), get out of that water, boy... you are going to drown." For seventeen years, I was taught by a loving and caring mother to fear the water. I adopted my mother's limitations as my own.

After joining the Army, I became excited about the possibility of becoming a Ranger. The Rangers or some of the toughest guys in the world and I wanted to be part of that great fellowship of warriors. The only problem with me joining the

Rangers was the most important thing...

"I could not swim."

THE TEST

The Ranger School swim test was not your typical swim test. Let me explain so that you can get a good mental picture of the larger than life task. The uniform for the swim test was as follows:

➢ Combat boots

➢ Full military uniform, paints & shirt

➢ Load bearing equipment with 2 canteens full of water & 2 ammunition pouches

➢ One M16 rifle (rubber)

The swim test consisted of these events:

➢ 15-meter swim

- 3-meter jump from a diving board & swim to the side

- Move away from the wall & drop all of your equipment and swim to the side.

I hope the information that I provide gives you a glimpse of my visible and invisible giants. Fear was my "invisible giant" but the swim test was my "visible giant". In 1980, I made my first attempt to pass the ranger school swim test. When I made the decision to move forward for the swim test at Fort Lewis Washington I went to a few of my army buddies for moral support and this is what happened. I went to an African American buddy of mine and told him my dream of becoming a Ranger and he promptly looked at me and said, "Johnson black guys don't swim".

Wow!!! Of course, this did absolutely nothing for my self-esteem or confidence. So, I proceeded to tell one of my other buddies about my dream, this buddy just happened to be a white guy. When I told my white army buddy about becoming a Ranger he said, "Johnson, black guys don't swim". At that point, I was getting low on confidence and my friends were about to steal my dream of becoming an Army Ranger.... Add naysayers to the list of giants!!

Prolonged association with negative people makes us think negatively, close contact with petty individuals develops petty habits in us. On the bright side, companionship with people with big ideas raises the level of our thinking; close contact with ambitious people gives us ambition....
-Dr. David J. Schwartz, Ph.D.
Think & Grow Rich

The big day came, and my squad leader takes me down to the pool for the test. I was beyond excited. However, in all of my excitement, I forgot a major aspect of this process... I hadn't trained or prepared for the events. I knew that there was a champion within me however the champion outside of me was not prepared. I thought my willpower would pull me through, boy... was I ever wrong. I failed, measurably and miserably. As a matter of fact, my squad leader had to pull me out of the water with a long pole with the hook on the end... the "Hook of Life" (**haha**). Let me give you a visual, water was going down my mouth and up my nose as I desperately tried to accomplish the mission of passing the Ranger swim test... with no preparation! However, **my failure was not final... there was still a champion inside of me.** It was at that time that I realized

I had to slay a few giants in my life. The champion within me became the **"Giant Killer."** Please get this... training and preparing spiritually, mentally, and physically, is the **sling-shot** needed to kill visible and invisible giants.

List the "Visible Giants" in your life:

_____

_____

_____

_____

List the Invisible Giants" in your life:

_____

_____

_____

_____

How have you allowed these giants hinder your dreams... your vision?

_____

_____

_____

_____

"Give me six hours to chop down a
tree and I will spend the first four
sharpening the axe"...
-Abraham Lincoln

When the student
is ready...
The teacher will appear!!

TODAYS PREPARATION

_____

_____

_____

_____

_____

_____

_____

_____

_____

_____

_____

CHAPTER 8

THE CHAMPION WITHIN

Failing the swim test made me want to be a Ranger even more. It was time to sharpen my Axe. So, I became driven to find out how to train for the event. After returning from Berlin Germany in 1984, while serving as a drill sergeant at Fort Benning Georgia, I was ready and the teacher appeared. Actually, I had two teachers, one was a female lifeguard, and the other was my drill sergeant buddy Dudley Carson (who was Ranger qualified and had served in the Ranger Battalion). I became driven to pass this swim test and spent count-less hours in the pool. Some days I struggled to learn the side stroke, but I had to continue

to believe in my dreams. After months and month of training, I finally became proficient enough to pass the test. As I stood on the side of that pool, I knew I was prepared.
I was grateful for another chance.

We live in a society programmed for instant gratification some of us really don't know what it's like to work for months or years for a goal or dream to come to fruition. So many people claim to want success but are lackluster in their preparation. Lack of preparation is the beginning of failing at any task. In our modern society, we can get instant oatmeal, instant grits and instant coffee and drive-thru restaurants. But you can't get instant success. As I stood on the edge of that ice cold pool in Ranger school, I can remember hearing the instructor say,

"Ranger... prepare to enter the water; enter the water". Just before I entered the water I thought of all of the hard work and dedication that led up to this moment and knew I was up for the challenge. I jumped in the pool with the weapon positioned in front of me and quickly sank a few feet under the surface. As my body came up and the weapon was visible I let out the loudest victory cry with the word... **"RANGER!!!!"**

Though I struggled to get beyond my fear of the water I kept my dreams out front. This time there was no need for the "jaws of life". I was prepared physically and mentally for the mission. Needless to say, I passed the swim test and became a U.S. Army Ranger. I had finally defeated my fear of the water. Finally, the adopted fear of my mother was long gone. My dream had come to life... I completed ranger school and graduated in Ranger Class 3-87 .... In this beautiful thing called life I have been blessed, but if you ask me what started it all it was **LEARNING TO SWIM**. When you develop the courage to attack your giants and beat them, it gives you an unbelievable amount of self-esteem and power. Still to this day, when people ask me, "what is the toughest thing you've ever done", I quickly reply, "learning to swim". Sometimes when life gets tough you have to revisit your "WHYS". I don't believe you can be great until you answer the "why" questions of your **GOALS** and **DREAMS**... Someone once said, "when your dream is big enough, the **how-to** won't matter." I'm not sure who said it, but I agree with it.

"Big dreams and hard work go hand in hand;
you can't fulfill your dreams without a
master plan...
The hunger pain of your dreams will truly tell
the story; infuse your dream with faith and
wait to see the glory.
Feed Your Dreams"
- J. Renee

The Ranger Creed

Recognizing that I volunteered as a Ranger, fully knowing the hazards of my chosen profession, I will always endeavor to uphold the prestige, honor, and high esprit de corps of my Ranger Regiment.

Acknowledging the fact that a Ranger is a more elite soldier who arrives at the cutting edge of battle by land, sea, or air, I accept the fact that as a Ranger my country expects me to move farther, faster and fight harder than any other soldier.

Never shall I fail my comrades. I will always keep myself mentally alert, physically strong and morally straight and I will shoulder more than my share of the task whatever it may be. One-hundred-percent and then some.

Gallantly will I show the world that I am a specially selected and well-trained soldier. My courtesy to superior officers, neatness of dress and care of equipment shall set the example for others to follow.

Energetically will I meet the enemies of my country. I shall defeat them on the field of battle for I am better trained and will fight with all my might. Surrender is not a Ranger word. I will never leave a fallen comrade to fall into the hands of the enemy and under no circumstances will I ever embarrass my country.

Readily will I display the intestinal fortitude required to fight on to the Ranger objective and complete the mission though I be the lone survivor.

RANGERS LEAD THE WAY!

As a Giant Killers and Champions, it is imperative that you are as prepared mentally as you are physically and spiritually. You can only become what the dominating thoughts in your mind tell you to become. So, only feed your mind with <u>pure</u>, <u>powerful</u> and <u>positive</u> information. "For as a man thinks within himself... so is he" (Proverbs 23:7) ...How you think about your dream has everything to do with the accomplishing of the dream. One of my favorite books is <u>The Magic of Thinking Big</u> by Dr. David J. Schwartz. Dr. Schwartz makes a great statement about an individual's attitude. The right attitude and one arm will beat the wrong attitude and two arms every day. So, little is given to attitude (or mindset) development in our society. I believe that the lack of sincere time and effort placed on developing a strong, mental attitude, as a society, has hurt us. However, we can recover... I don't have a big scientific study to throw at you, nor can I spout off numbers and show graphs and charts on good vs. bad attitudes....

I just know what I know..

- When you change your outlook,

  you change your life...

- When you change your perspective,

  you change your position...

- When you change your position,

  you change your performance...

- When you change your performance,

  you change your world...

- When you change your world,

  you change my life...

This sounds like the formula for making a

CHAMPION!!!

Now the question is... when will change

happen for you??? Pastor Mark Hankins gives

3 reasons or seasons that can lead to change...

> **When they hurt badly enough that they have to...**

> **When the rewards are great enough that they want to...**

> **When they learn enough that they are able to...**

The Shaquem Griffin Story...
A Burning Desire to Win

A **burning desire** to win is the statement

that comes to mind when thinking about

<u>Shaquem Griffin.</u> Shaquem Griffin is the football player who was picked in the fifth-round of the 2018 NFL draft. Shaquem is the twin brother of Shaquill Griffin (who was also picked in the 2017 draft). Though they were born just minutes apart, Shaquem was born with what appeared to be a disadvantage. If you are unfamiliar with this story let me quickly update you.

Shaquem was born with a congenital condition called amniotic band syndrome. This syndrome stunted the development of his left arm and caused excruciating pain and at the age of 4, Griffin's left hand was amputated. Although the diagnosis presented itself as an opposition, I believe that it was fuel that gave him a **burning desire to win.** I also believe that his ability to overcome his obstacle gave

many others permission to stay in the fight in

the game called life. Griffin has become an

inspiration for other limb-deficient athletes. He

has also become an inspiration to onlookers

and passersby. Griffin seemed to reject the

the idea that he was at a disadvantage, and

used adversity as fuel to win. I would say that

he saw a setback as a means to a comeback.

While watching interviews of the Griffin family,

you could see how they pushed their sons with

love and support; it wasn't all about football.

His parents never allowed him to adopt the

limitations of others as his own. Griffin's

parents made sure that he trained and

prepared for the challenges ahead of him. His

lack of a limb became the thing that produced

perseverance, endurance and tenacity. It seems that his loving, supportive, environment and his burning desire to win was very instrumental in his successful football journey. A desire will take you much farther than knowledge. Why? Because knowledge is limited to what you know. I believe your desire is tied to something deep down inside of you that say's "I can do it---No I will do it."

The twins chose to attend the University of Central Florida because it was the program that understood that they were a "package deal". Shaquill (a cornerback) was drafted by the Seahawks with the 90th pick, in the third round of the 2017 draft. This was the first season that the twins spent apart. During the

2017 season, Shaquill started 11 games for the Seahawks while his twin brother Shaquem, who red-shirted as a freshman, helped lead UCF to an undefeated season. Living on opposite coasts prepared them for what they thought was the "inevitability" of playing on different NFL teams.

The Seahawks took Shaquem with the No. 141 pick, four selections into the fifth round, a special-teams player who will work in at weak side linebacker on the same defense as his brother. The Griffin brothers will have an opportunity to play together again and we will have another opportunity to witness a burning desire to love and to win. He believed he could and he did.

OVERCOME YOUR OBSTACLES...

FULFILL YOUR DREAMS

I hope that as I shared how I overcame obstacles and roadblocks in my life, you will be able to gain inspiration and revelation to do the same. Though inspiration and motivation can get you going, it's the revelation that keeps us GROWING. It has been said that change is inevitable, but GROWTH is intentional...So, I encourage you to be intentional about dreaming and be intentional about doing the necessary thing to help those dreams come to life. Train like you fight by preparing today for tomorrow's mission...

"Work while they sleep.
Learn while they party.
Save while they spend.
Live like they dream."

— Anonymous

TODAYS PREPARATION

What is the toughest thing you have accomplished?

_____

_____

What giant are you still battling?

_____

_____

_____

What is your plan of action to win?

_____

_____

_____

Have you been tentative or intentional about winning?

_____

How do you plan to change or improve from this day forth?

_____

_____

_____

TRAINING STRATEGIES

➢ **Plan your day**

> **Structure produces traction and produces forward movement...**

➢ **Find a Mentor**

➢ **Use a calendar and notebook for daily assignments**

➢ **Write your vision**

➢ **Expand your circle of friends with those of similar, positive, visions...**

**If you are the smartest in your circle, you need to expand your circle...
In order to become successful, it requires an enormous amount of energy. Negative images, surroundings, and life styles drain the positive life force needed to climb this mountain called productivity.**

Most people spend more time planning their vacation than they do planning their life. There are also many time stealers that will take away from your planning time. TV is a major enemy of would be successful people. I heard a statistic last week that blows me away. The average person in America watches 8 hours of TV per day, but the average millionaire only watches 1 hour of TV per day. According to Cheryl Sherry a *Post-Crescent staff writer* on average, children in the United States will spend more time in front of the television **(1,023)** than in school this year **(900 hours)**. Plan your day like your life depends on it because it does. One of my favorite people to study planning from is MARY KAY ASH the founder of Mary Kay Cosmetics. Someone once asked Mary Kay how did she develop her plans and stay focused each day? The answer she gave was so simple yet powerful.

Mary Kay's (Daily Success Plan)

Before I start working I write down the top 6 things I need to accomplish that day and number them from 1 the most important to 6 the least important. As I go through my day I stay focused on completing the things on my list in the order of their importance. I believe we can all learn from a great visionary like Mary Kay Ash.   Over the years I have heard many speakers say "plan your work and work your plan" but many haven't been able to verbalize the plan, so you can see it as Mary Kay has.

Find a Mentor

Before we dive into the subject of mentors let's spend some time developing the word *MENTOR*. We need to better understand what it means to have a mentor or become a mentor. I believe this to be one of the biggest secrets to becoming successful in any career, job, business, or profession. Mentor is a word used so much in our culture today and I am amazed

that we don't have more successful Dreamers...
When I was a young Private E-1 in the army,
stationed at Fort Lewis Washington, I can
remember my First Sergeant writing notes as
we went to him for advice and counsel. One
day I ask First Sergeant Sloan why he always
wrote things down and his answer was pure
gold and wisdom to my young ears.

First Sergeant Sloan's WISDOM

"Private Johnson, no man can remember
everything that must be done in a day and your
mind / memory will fail you at the critical
moment." 1st Sgt. Sloan was a Vietnam
Vet with a lot of combat experience, so I took
him at his word and he became my first mentor
for planning. I don't believe that one person
can be your mentor for everything in life
because no one person is a master at
everything. Your pastor might be your spiritual
mentor and they will serve you well in this
capacity but not as a physical fitness coach.

Your physical fitness coach may serve you well while teaching you push-ups and sit-ups, but they know very little about finance and investments. Seek God for wisdom and guidance for mentorship. You will know them when you see them.

A MENTOR IS NOT SOMEONE THAT YOU LISTEN TO; A MENTOR IS SOMEONE THAT YOU FOLLOW THEIR ADVICE...
-MIKE MURDOCK

1st Sgt. Sloan taught me how to be more effective in planning my daily assignments.... I began writing down each one of my daily assignments for the upcoming day before I went to bed at night. Having a calendar and a notebook became a part my training. Only 3 people out of 100 actually plan their day. A calendar and a notebook will move you so far ahead of the crowd of people that are waiting for life to happen to them. They **wish** instead of **dream**!! Now, my leadership mentor was all together different. Mike Jefferson was the epitome of leadership. He would get to work early and leave late, he always had a can-do attitude. Mike became a great mentor for me. We met at a time when I was looking for a guy who could take me to the next level of leadership. I remember one of my first encounters with this big strong guy..."Iron Mike". Mike had the presence and persona of a man on a mission. I walked into the Company one day and Mike was hitting his punching bag with reckless abandon. This immediately won my respect. Mike was a Sergeant Major, the senior ranking enlisted guy in our Special Forces Company. As a senior leader Mike didn't just talk the talk he walked the walk. He led by example. Mike had instant creditability and respect with the other warriors in our company because he was in great shape and he had **IT**. I don't know how to explain **IT** ...I just know **IT** when I see **IT**.

Every person that desires greatness should have an opportunity to sit at a great leaders' feet while learning. The Mike warrior spirit about him was contagious. Mike inherited a Unit that was in a mess... The previous leader didn't value preparation and training...and it was exhibited through his character. Once Mike took over the Unit, his leadership style helped us to buy into the attitude of' Train Like You Fight" ... Our organization went to the top. Many people don't believe that one person can make a difference, but I beg to differ. One very negative person or very positive person can have a dramatic effect on a group of people. Mike's "Train like You Fight" attitude spread throughout our company and we soon became one of the best Units in Special Forces.

"Never doubt that one
person can make a difference..."
-Ingrid Newkirk

Refer back to your dream board in chapter 4 and answer these questions.

1. Why do I desire this?

_____

_____

_____

_____

_____

2. What is there to gain?

_____

_____

_____

_____

3. Is this a worthy goal?

_____

_____

_____

4. Why must I see this vision/dream through to the end?

_____

_____

_____

_____

_____

5. How can I help others as I accomplish my goal?

_____

_____

_____

_____

_____

"When you have been
Strengthened, strengthen you brother" ...
(Luke 22:32)

JOURNAL

JOURNAL

JOURNAL

JOURNAL

My purpose must always be pointed toward
fulfilling Gods Mission for my life...
Terry "Ranger" Johnson

My life is worth nothing to me unless I use it
for finishing the work assigned me by the
Lord Jesus....
Acts 20:24(NLT)

REFERENCES

Note: The transitions used for most scriptures are as marked, KJV used otherwise. (The Holy Bible...TPT, MSG)

The Magic of Thinking Big …..David J. Schwartz

Think & Grow Rich………… Napoleon Hill

Royalty-That's How…………. Renee M. Johnson
He Sees Me

The Portable Pep Talk……… Alexander Lockhart

The New………………Mark and Trina Hankins

Shaquem Griffin Story ………..
http://www.dailymagazine.news/shaquem-griffin-s-nfl-story-begins-now-nid-589812.html

ABOUT THE AUTHOR
Terry "Ranger" Johnson

He enlisted in the U.S. Army on June 10, 1980 and retired from the military in June 2000 with 20 years of service. Terry developed his unique leadership style while serving in some of the most elite units in the Army. He spent the last 11 years of his career serving in the Special Forces. As a Special Forces soldier (Green Beret), he conducted nation building operations in South and Central America.

Terry has always had a tremendous love for teaching and empowering others. He believes that "to whom much is given much is required." This love for others led him and his wife (Renee) to develop "The ChampionsWithin Kingdom Builders". Champions Within helps develop and build leaders in churches, schools, businesses, and correctional facilities around the nation.

Terry is from Marietta, Texas and married to the former Renee Minor of Rayville, Louisiana. Renee is also an author.

For booking information please contact us at:
E-mail: championswithin@yahoo.com
www.rangerjohnson.com
U.S. Army Retired
Ranger / Green Beret